I Have Lunch

Dona Herweck Rice

Library of Congress Cataloging-in-Publication Data

Names: Rice, Dona, author.
Title: I have lunch / Dona Herweck Rice.
Description: Huntington Beach, CA : Teacher Created Materials, Inc., [2019] | Audience: Age 4-6. |
Identifiers: LCCN 2018020230 (print) | LCCN 2018021450 (ebook) | ISBN 9781493898954 () | ISBN 9781493898213 (pbk.)
Subjects: LCSH: Lunchbox cooking--Juvenile literature. | Luncheons--Juvenile literature. | School children--Food--Juvenile literature. | LCGFT: Cookbooks.
Classification: LCC TX735 (ebook) | LCC TX735 .R49 2019 (print) | DDC 641.5/3--dc23
LC record available at https://lccn.loc.gov/2018020230

Publishing Credits

Rachelle Cracchiolo, M.S.Ed., *Publisher*
Conni Medina, M.A.Ed., *Managing Editor*
Nika Fabienke, Ed.D., *Content Director*
Véronique Bos, *Creative Director*
Shaun N. Bernadou, *Art Director*
Carol Huey-Gatewood, M.A.Ed., *Editor*
Valerie Morales, *Associate Editor*
Courtney Roberson, *Senior Graphic Designer*

Image Credits: All images from iStock and/or Shutterstock.

Teacher Created Materials
5301 Oceanus Drive
Huntington Beach, CA 92649-1030
www.tcmpub.com

ISBN 978-1-4938-9821-3

I have  .

bread

I have 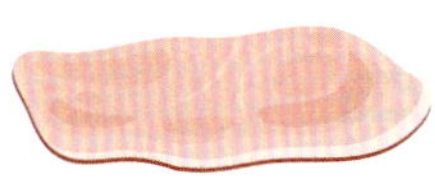 .

ham

I have  .

cheese

I have  .

lettuce

I have  .

chips

I have  .

milk

I have  .

carrots

I have  .

grapes

I have  .

cookies

I have  .

lunch

High-Frequency Words

have

I